HEARING THEIR PREY

ANIMALS WITH AN AMAZING SENSE OF HEARING

written by Kathryn Lay
illustrated by Christina Wald

visit us at www.abdopublishing.com

Published by Magic Wagon, a division of the ABDO Group, PO Box 398166, Minneapolis, MN 55439.
Copyright © 2013 by Abdo Consulting Group, Inc. International copyrights reserved in all countries. All rights
reserved. No part of this book may be reproduced in any form without written permission from the publisher.

Looking Glass Library™ is a trademark and logo of Magic Wagon.

Printed in the United States of America, North Mankato, Minnesota.
052012
092012

Written by Kathryn Lay
Illustrated by Christina Wald
Edited by Stephanie Hedlund and Rochelle Baltzer
Cover and interior layout and design by Neil Klinepier

Library of Congress Cataloging-in-Publication Data

Lay, Kathryn.
  Hearing their prey : animals with an amazing sense of hearing / written by Kathryn Lay ; illustrated by Christina
Wald.
    p. cm. -- (Sensing their prey)
  Includes index.
  ISBN 978-1-61641-866-3
  1. Hearing--Juvenile literature. 2. Senses and sensation--Juvenile literature. 3. Animal behavior--Juvenile
literature. I. Wald, Christina, ill. II. Title.
  QP462.2.L39 2013
  612.8'5--dc23
                            2011052273

CONTENTS

Can You Hear Your Dinner?

Have you ever seen a fox open a refrigerator? Or spotted a lion in line at the grocery store? Or watched an owl ask its mom for a peanut butter and jelly sandwich?

Animals must find their own food every day. A predator is an animal that lives by eating other animals. Many predators have strong senses that help them. Some animals use their sense of hearing to find their prey.

Hearing Far Away

A wolf can hear sound as far as six miles (10 km) away in the forest. In open country, it can hear ten miles (16 km) away. When it is sleeping, a wolf's ears stand straight up to hear other animals making sounds.

Do your ears stick up when your breakfast is cooking? When you are playing at a friend's house, can you hear your dad grilling at home?

Hear Prey Underground

A fox has such a strong sense of hearing that it can hunt animals that are underground! Sometimes, its prey is buried deep down in the ground. The fox can zoom in on where the sound is coming from. Then, it quickly digs out mice, rabbits, and insects.

Can you find your lunch deep down in your backpack by hearing it?

Finding Food Without Looking

Owls have the best hearing ability of all birds. Their ears are hidden by feathers. Yet, they can hear so well that they do not have to see their prey to know it is around.

If you closed your eyes, could you find your dinner and know what it was by listening to it?

An owl's ears are at the side of the head behind the eyes. The front of an owl's face is round like a disk. This feathery disk helps funnel sound to its ears.

Understanding Many Sounds at One Time

All cats, including house cats and big cats, have excellent hearing. Cats can tell the difference between more than 100 sounds, all at the same time!

How many different sounds can you hear when you are on the playground? How about in the school cafeteria?

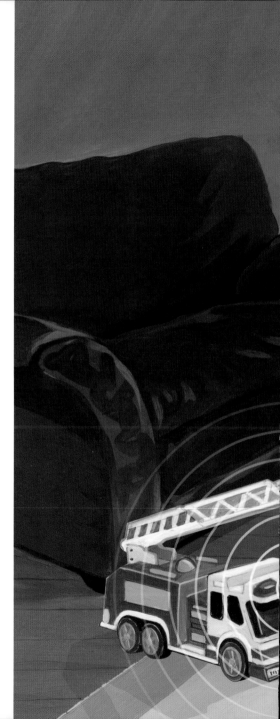

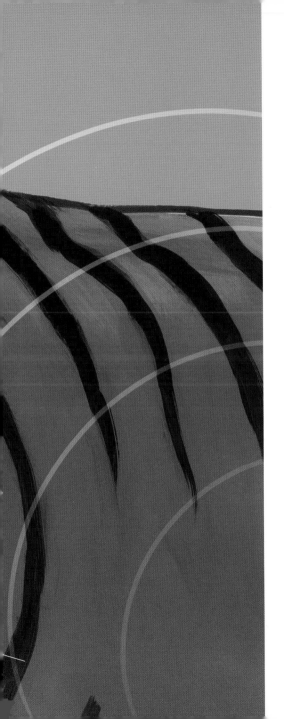

Movable Ears

Like other cats, a tiger swivels its ears to find its prey. It may twist just one ear to listen to a sound. It might even move both ears in slightly different directions. Tigers use their amazing hearing to find prey even in thick bushes.

Could you find your lunch in the middle of tall grass by listening? Can you make your ears move without touching them?

EAR SHAPE FOR BETTER HEARING

A dog's ears twitch and turn when it hears sounds. Wild dogs have large ears that are almost round, giving them excellent hearing.

What shape are your ears? What about your friends' ears?

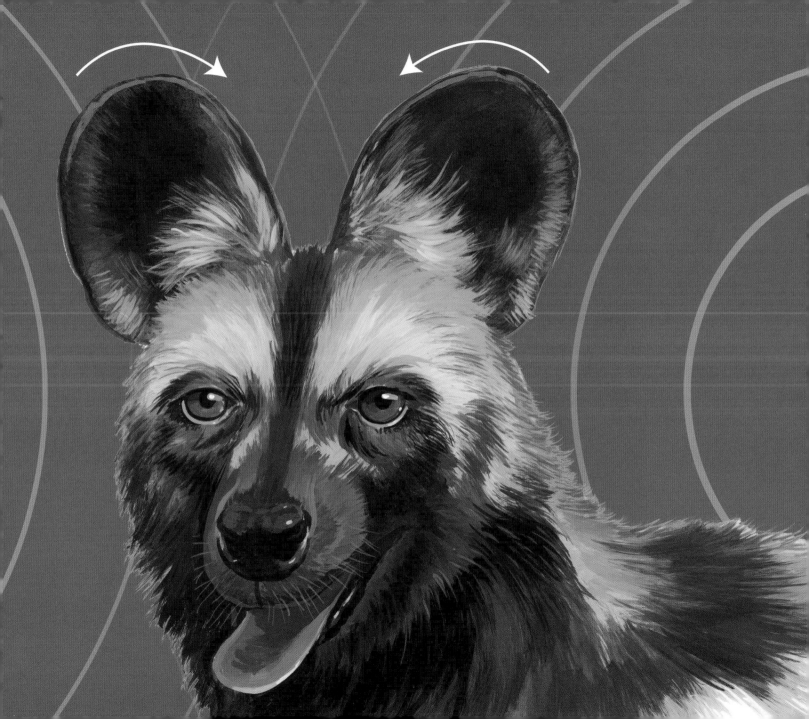

R-RACK-K-K

A Bear of a Hearing Test

Have you ever had a hearing test? Scientists did a special hearing test on polar bears. They learned that the bears can hear both low-frequency and high-frequency sounds equally well.

Hearing Help

Have you seen someone who wears a hearing aid to hear better? The lynx's hearing is helped by tufts of hair on its ears. These tufts guide sound to the ears. They act almost like hearing aids!

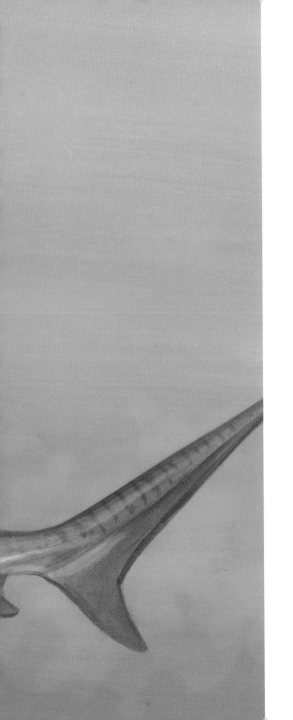

Underwater Hearing

With well-developed inner ears, sharks can pick up sounds up to 1,700 yards (1,600 m) away. Sound travels better and farther in water than in air. Sharks are especially attracted to low-frequency sounds like the ones made by a wounded fish.

Can you hear something that is 1,700 yards (1,600 m) away? That is more than 14 football fields away!

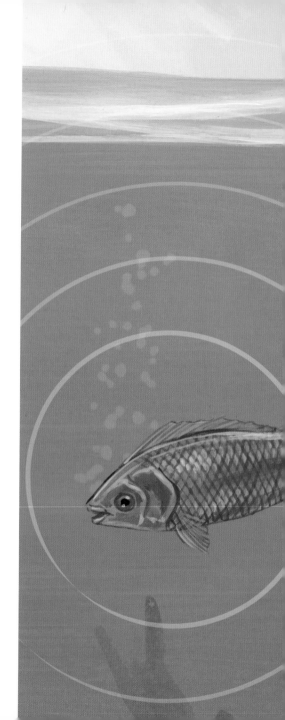

Shaky Hearing

The matamata turtle in the Amazon basin has special eardrums. These eardrums help the turtle detect the vibrations of their prey's movements in the water.

If you are swimming underwater, can you hear your friend walking around you?

Without their amazing hearing, many predators would not be able to find food. Do you hear your stomach growling? Maybe you are hungry, too!

GLOSSARY

basin - the land drained by a river and its connected streams.

funnel - to move through a narrow passage.

high-frequency - sound vibrations that are fast, creating a high note.

low-frequency - sound vibrations that are slow, creating a low note.

swivel - to freely turn or twist.

tuft - a small patch of feathers or hair that grows close together.

twitch - to move with sudden motion.

vibration - tiny back-and-forth movements.

INDEX

WEB SITES

To learn more about animal senses, visit ABDO Group online at **www.abdopublishing.com**. Web sites about animal senses are featured on our Book Links page. These links are routinely monitored and updated to provide the most current information available.